Spring 1982   Volume V Number 1

Paperback Quarterly

"Journal of
Mass-Market Paperback History"

Contents

Paperback Quarterly Publications
Brownwood, Texas

Paperback Quarterly specializes in the history of mass market paperbacks. *Paperback Quarterly* features articles and notes dealing with every type (mystery, detective, science fiction, western, adventure, etc) and with every aspect of new old and rare paperbacks.

Emphasis is placed on the historical research of paperbacks, their authors, illustrators, publishers and distributors, but the editors also invite contributions of bibliographical interest. In short, the only criterion for the editors' consideration is that the subject matter pertain to paperbacks.

Paperback Quarterly pays 2¢ per word (200-2000 words) for articles and notes. Payment also includes two copies of the issue in which your article appears.

Paperback quarterly is published in spring, summer, fall and winter of each year with a subscription rate of $10.00 per year or individual copies for $3.50 each. Institutional and library subscriptions are $12.00 per year. Overseas rate is $15.00. All back issues are out of print.

All correspondence, articles, notes, queries, ads and subscriptions should be sent to 1710 Vincent, Brownwood, Texas 76801. (915) 643-1182. Ad rate card on request.

Published and Edited by

Charlotte Laughlin   Billy C. Lee

Contributing Editors

Bill Crider   Michael S. Barson
William Lyles   Thomas L. Bonn
Piet Schreuders

Printer and Technical Advisor
Martin E. Gottschalk

Copy Editor
Judy Crider

Cover logo designed by Peter Manesis

Cover art from: (top center) *The Heart Remembers*, Dell #288; (right) *The Heart Has April Too*, Dell #373--drawn by Harry Bennett; (left) *Strangers May Kiss*, Dell #409--drawn by Ray Johnson.

Pink for La Vie En Rose:
Early Dell Romances
by Angela Andrews

After World War II the emphasis on paperback books for women readers changed. Heroic
and patriotic themes had been exhausted and
were replaced by those of love and romance.
The goggled welder's hood worn by Augusta
Clawson and described by her in SHIPYARD DIARY
OF A WOMAN WELDER (Penguin Special S218) was
forsaken for those rose-tinted spectacles so
beloved of heroines in the increasingly popular
romances now being reprinted in paperback, and
written by such favorite authors as Faith
Baldwin, Olive Higgins Prouty, LIda Larrimore
and Maysie Greig.

The early post-war period was a time of
austerity, not only in ruined Europe but in
America as well. Working principally in
offices, factories and hospitals, women who had
contributed to the war effort now, for economic
reasons, continued to be a significant part of
the labor force after the War. Faith Baldwin's
THE OFFICE WIFE (Pocket Book #150), WHITE COLLAR
GIRL (Pocket Book #311), and WIFE VS. SECRETARY
(Dell #12) reflected this social change from
housewife to worker. It was at this time that
the curious concept of the "office wife" came
into being. There is actually an article entitled "How to Pick An Office Wife," found in a
women's magazine of 1942. It begins: "She can
make you or break you--that office wife with
whom you will spend most of your working hours--
so choose her with care...she must feel that
[her boss's] affairs are so important that it is
a pleasure to go without her lunch-hour and
nibble a sandwich at her desk when pressure is
high...." A nurse also was supposed to carry
out the handsome doctor's command, as a wife
traditionally had deferred to her husband's.

Dell Romances

This encouragement to the working woman to put not only effort but also emotion into her job could not have been entirely satisfactory for her. Gladys Taber, another writer of this time, wrote in her "Diary of Domesticity" for the LADIES HOME JOURNAL: "We are always pursuing happiness and security. Now and then, rarely we find them, if only briefly." Surely it was this elusive hope of something better on the horizon that helped most women through their everyday routines during this grey and difficult post-war time, rather than a pat on the head—or worse—from their employer!

Having successfully published for twenty-five years such true love magazines as SCREEN ROMANCES and MODERN ROMANCES as well as BEST DETECTIVE, DELL CROSSWORD PUZZLES, LOONEY TUNES and many others, this experience together with an understanding of what people liked to read, gave George T. Delacorte, Jr., and his Dell Publishing Company considerable advantage over other paperback publishers when, in 1942, with the Western Printing & Lithography Company of Poughkeepsie, Dell began publishing paperback books.

After eleven mysteries, Dell #12 was the first Dell Romance. "This is a Dell Book presenting a new exciting popular series selected by the editors of America's foremost fiction magazines," was printed on the back cover. WIFE VS. SECRETARY by Faith Baldwin was a fairly safe choice as her THE OFFICE WIFE had been published earlier by Pocket Books in 1942. The cover of Dell #12 shows a pink wife figure in outline, overlapped by the secretary, an envious green. With pencil and notebook in one hand, the secretary strides purposefully in the opposite direction from the wife.

When the second Dell Romance appeared (Samuel Hopkins Adams' TAMBAY GOLD (Dell #20), it was apparent that the romantic cover design format had not yet been perfected. An early

5

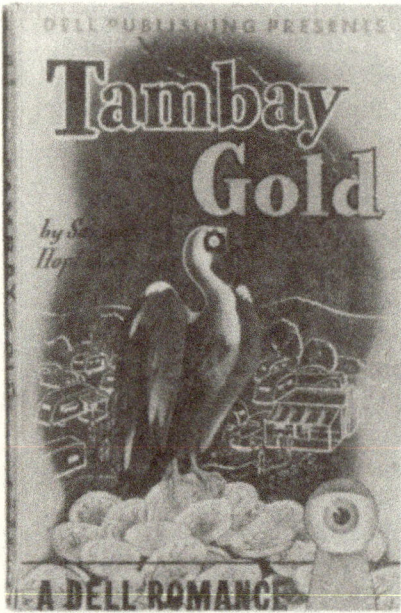

Dell Romances

mapback, the cover reveals an unromantic vulture
complete with red and baleful eye, settled on a
hoard of golden treasure.

The third paperback in the new romantic
series was another wife-secretary dilemma by
Faith Baldwin. Entitled WEEK-END MARRIAGE
(Dell #73), the book has two suitcases on the
cover--one with a piece of purple negligee
showing. The cases are encircled--almost
imprisoned--by a thick gold wedding band.
Although this was not a very carefree cover
either, for the first time a small red heart
replaced the usual Dell "eye-in-the-keyhole"
colophon. However, it was not until 1946 with
the appearance of NOW VOYAGER by Olive Higgins
Prouty (Dell #99) that romance quite literally
began to blossom: a ship floating away on a
heart-shaped ocean, enveloped in blushing
camellia petals set the pattern for Dell Romance covers that was to continue till 1952,
when the popularity of the romance began to
wane. Possibly the last Dell Romance of this
type and era was FABIA by Olive Higgins Prouty
(Dell #648). The time span of these Dell
Romances coincides almost exactly with the fall
and recovery of the American economy.

While it lasted this was a unique selection
of light romances that were successfully inter-
woven between the more predominant mysteries
and murders. With at least one heart on every
cover, every other conceivable symbol of romance also came to be represented in this series.
As well as camellias and roses, stars and moons,
there were champagne glasses with plentiful
bubbles; lace and cupids, an angel, and, symbol-
izing everlasting happiness, bride and bride-
groom couples in formal attire, the size of
wedding-cake decorations. There were, as well,
E. M. Hull's dashing "Sheik" desert romances,
reviving fond memories of Rudolph Valentino.

By the early 1950s, however, Dell's light
romances made way for more unbridled and pas-

MAYSIE GREIG

Reluctant Millionaire

A DELL ROMANCE

KIND ARE HER ANSWERS

A DELL ROMANCE

Golden EARRINGS

by YOLANDA FOLDES

A DELL ROMANCE

TEMPLE BAILEY

THE Pink Camellia

A DELL ROMANCE

Dell Romances

8

sionate fiction; and the westerns and mysteries were tougher, too, heralding the beginning of the "sex, sin, and smoking gun" era.

George Delacorte, still attuned to what people wanted to read, prospered in the paperback boom of the 1950s; and, by 1963, Dell had become one of the leading paperback publishers in the United States. Although the light romances vanished, their popularity in the late 1940s and early 1950s undoubtedly contributed to Dell's success.

Now, nearly forty years since the first Dell Romance was published, the American economy is lean once again. In bookstores, alongside Fawcett's Coventry Romances, and those of Harlequin and Silhouette, large supplies of Dell's Candlelight and Ecstasy Romances can be seen. As before, Dell Romances are holding their own in troubled times.

Following is a checklist of Dell Romances; additions would be welcomed.

Dell #12 WIFE VS. SECRETARY by Faith Baldwin
     #20 TAMBAY GOLD by Samuel Hopkins Adams
     #73 WEEKEND MARRIAGE by Faith Baldwin
     #99 NOW, VOYAGER by Olive Higgins Prouty
    #116 HONOR BOUND by Faith Baldwin
    #117 WOMEN ARE LIKE THAT by Alice Elinor
             Lambert
    #118 HALF ANGEL by Fanny Heaslip Lea
    #119 ROBIN HILL by Lida Larrimore
    #138 MEN ARE SUCH FOOLS by Faith Baldwin
    #139 LOVE AND THE COUNTESS TO BOOT by
             Jack Iams
    #140 FOOT PRINT OF CINDERELLA by Philip
             Wylie
    #141 THE SWIFT HOUR by Hariett Thurman
    #163 SELF-MADE WOMAN by Faith Baldwin
    #167 WHITE FAWN by Olive H ggins Prouty
    #170 RELUCTANT MILLIONAIRE by Maysie Greig
    #174 THE SHEIK by E. M. Hull
    #178 THE PINK CAMELLIA by Temple Bailey

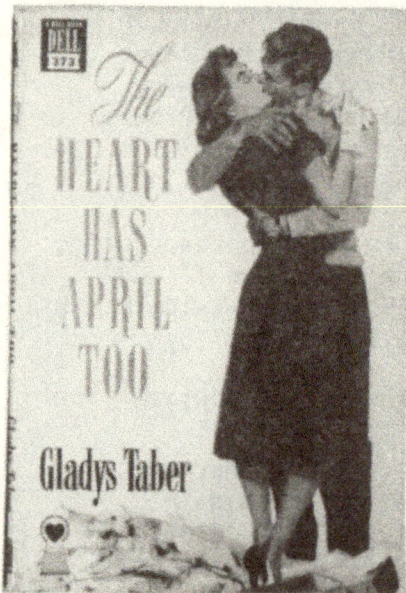

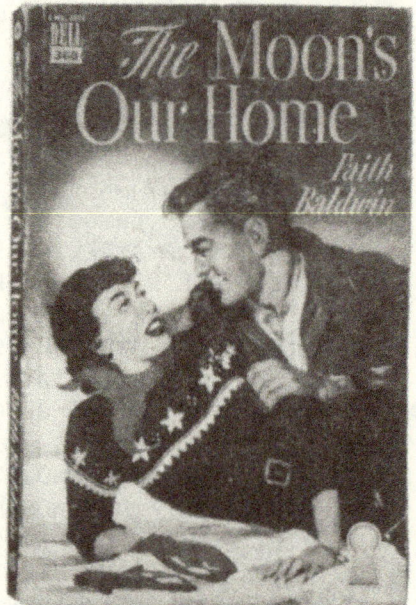

Dell Romances

#183 AMERICAN ACRES by Louise Redfield
          Peattie
#188 THE SPLENDID QUEST by Edison Marshall
#189 KIND ARE HER ANSWERS by Mary Renault
#196 RICH GIRL, POOR GIRL by Faith Baldwin
#216 GOLDEN EARRINGS by Yolanda Foldes
#220 HOSPITAL NOCTURNE by Alice Elinor
          Lambert
#234 STUDENT NURSE by Renee Shann
#236 SKYSCRAPER by Faith Baldwin
#239 CANDIDATE FOR LOVE by Maysie Greig
#245 WALLFLOWERS by Temple Bailey
#249 STARS STILL SHINE by Lida Larrimore
#255 ENCHANTED OASIS by Faith Baldwin
#279 SONS OF THE SHEIK by E. M. Hull
#288 THE HEART REMEMBERS by Faith Baldwin
#298 PROMISE OF LOVE by Mary Renault
#309 SATIN STRAPS by Maysie Greig
#318 ALIMONY by Faith Baldwin
#336 AFTERGLOW by Ruby M. Ayres
#342 SONS OF THE SHEIK by E. M. Hull
#368 THE MOON'S OUR HOME by Faith Baldwin
#373 THE HEART HAS APRIL TOO by Gladys
          Taber
#402 THE CAPTIVE OF THE SAHARA by E. M.
          Hull
#445 THE HIGH ROAD by Faith Baldwin
#446 YOURS EVER by Maysie Greig
#475 MANHATTAN NIGHTS by Faith Baldwin
#496 WHISPERS IN THE SUN by Maysie Greig
#532 THE INCREDIBLE YEAR by Faith Baldwin
#574 FOR RICHER, FOR POORER by Faith
          Baldwin
#648 FABIA by Live Higgins Prouty

References:

"Dell, Publishers of Magazines and Reprints,"
     PUBLISHERS WEEKLY, May 19, 1954.
"George T. Delacorte, Jr." CURRENT BIOGRAPHY,
     1965, pp. 111-113.
"Gladys Taber," CURRENT BIOGRAPHY, 1965, pp. 574-

575.
Palmer, Gretta. "How to Pick an Office Wife,"
CORONET, Vol. 12, No. 4, August 1942.

Conan in Paperback
by Charlotte Laughlin

Although everybody these days is talking about Conan on film, Conan in paperback has been popular since the late 1960s. And the publishing history of some of the paperbacks is as tangled as the adventures experienced by the Barbarian himself.

The first Conan paperback is Ace D-36, CONAN THE CONQUEROR, published in 1953, with a cover painting by Norman Saunders (see PQ Vol. I, No. 3). A huge ax in an executioner's block dominates the foreground, behind which Conan brandishes a sword in one hand and holds a scantily clad damsel in distress in the other. He is dressed as a Roman centurian rather than as a barbarian; and both Conan and the damsel look very Anglo-Saxon, not Celtic. This Ace edition (an Ace double novel bound together with THE SWORD OF RHIANNON by Leigh Brackett) is a reprint of the Gnome Press hardback edited by John D. Clark and published in 1950. Clark took as his original the five serials published in WEIRD TALES, December 1935-April 1936, under the title THE HOUR OF THE DRAGON.

Howard had prepared THE HOUR OF THE DRAGON for British hardback publication, at the request of Denis Archer, a Pawling and Ness editor, for a novel-length manuscript instead of a collection of short stories. Howard received the request in January of 1934, hurriedly cannibalized many of his own stories that had previously appeared in WEIRD TALES, and sent the manuscript, titled THE HOUR OF THE DRAGON, to Archer in May of 1934. Pawling and Ness accepted the manuscript but folded before publishing it. Howard salvaged his work by selling it serially to WEIRD TALES, which thus repurchased and republished the material it had used earlier in a slightly different form.[1]

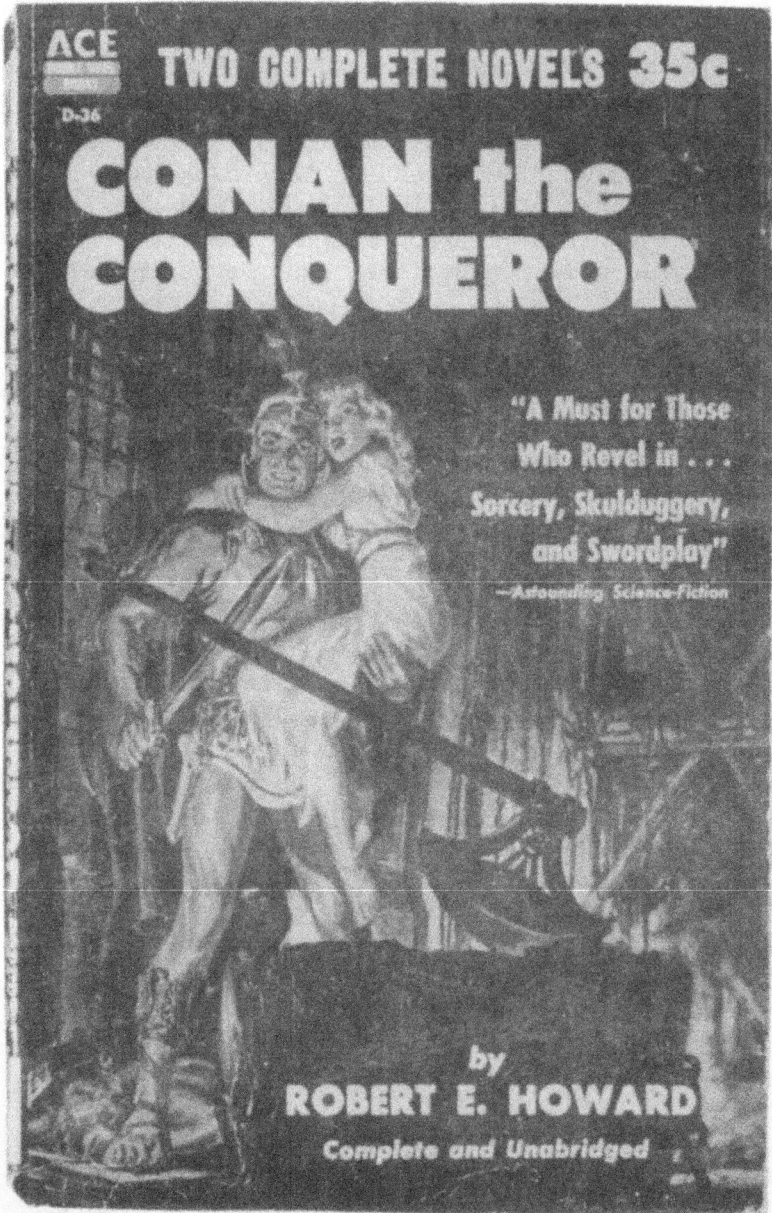

Conan's first paperback appearance, Ace D-36, 1953

14

After D-36, CONAN THE CONQUEROR did not
again appear in an Ace edition until 1977, when
it was published as volume nine in the Ace chronological series. Between those Ace editions,
it was published in two editions for Lancer,
which created today's image of Conan by bring-
ing Conan and Frank Frazetta together. Lancer
commissioned Frazetta to do cover paintings for
the first six and the last Conan titles it issued; and these covers, which have practically
defined the character of Conan for a generation
of readers, were also used for the 1977 Ace series.

John Milius, writer/director of the current movie CONAN THE BARBARIAN, says, "Frank
Frazetta is the high priest of Conan. We were
aware of this all the time we were shooting the
film. He certainly was an influence on me.
Frazetta's Conan illustrations were more important to me than the books were."

The film's production designer, Ron Cobb,
at first resisted the reliance on Frazetta's
imagery. "I didn't want to go that way at all.
...It seemed to me that the picture needed a
fresh viewpoint, because Frazetta has become a
cliche. But Milius saw Frazetta as the arche-
typal image of Conan, and he was right."[2]

As definitive as these Frazetta paintings
are considered to be by some fans and collectors, Berkley Medallion commissioned a new
painting for its 1977 edition of CONAN THE
CONQUEROR, edited by Karl Edward Wagner and
published under the original title THE HOUR OF
THE DRAGON.

Thus, collectors of Conan in paperback
have copies of CONAN THE CONQUEROR to obtain:
Ace D-36; Lancer 73-572 (1967) "Volume Three of
the Complete Conan"; Lancer 75137 (1970) "Volume Five in the Saga of Fantasy-Adventure's
Mightiest Hero"; "Ace 11679 (1977) volume nine
in Ace's chronological series; and Berkley
Medallion 0-425-036081 (1977) "The Authorized

Bob Larkin

Boris

Conan pastiches by L. Sprague de Camp & Lin Carter

Edition," titled THE HOUR OF THE DRAGON.

The numbering of the various Lancer editions is confusing to collector and bibliographer alike. The first five titles issued
by Lancer were given a number printed in small
letters on the front cover. I haven't seen the
sixth, ninth, or tenth title; but the seventh
and eighth have no volume number given on the
cover or title-page. The eleventh title (CONAN
THE BUCCANEER, #75-181, 1971) has no volume
number on the cover but carries this statement
on the title-page: "Number Eleven in the Lancer
Uniform Edition of CONAN. Chronologically this
volume is Number Six in the Saga of CONAN, following CONAN THE ADVENTURER and preceding CONAN
THE WARRIOR."

In 1970, Lancer issued the Conan novels in
a new series with different numbers. These
editions used the same cover paintings as the
earlier Lancer editions but changed the format
of the headings on the books. The new format

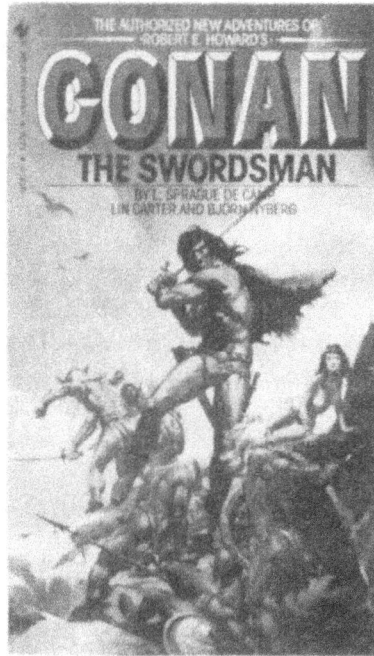

(Lancer, 1966)   (Bantam, 1981)

has an inch-and-a-half strip of color at the
top of each book. A numeral to indicate the
new volume number is centered in the colored
strip; and to the left of the numeral is the
phrase, "Volume ____ in the Saga of Fantasy-
Adventure's Mightiest Hero."

It would be nice to say that in 1970 Lancer
changed the format of its Conan series and that
the books printed thereafter were in the new
format. Unfortunately, the tangled publishing
history of Lancer Books is not nearly so neat.
Also in 1970, CONAN THE ADVENTURER was republished with a new number (75-102) and new price
(95¢), but like the 1966 edition (73-526),
which sold for 60¢, it was in the old format
and described as "Volume One of the Complete
Conan."

By Number Three in the new series, Lancer
was including a list of the Conan novels in
chronological order facing the title-page. This
list is in the same order as the later Ace series.

By Number Six in the new series (still 1970) Lancer was including a note on the title-page to explain the difference in Conan's chronological order and the series order: "Number Six in the Lancer Uniform Edition of CONAN. Chronologically this volume is Number Twelve in the Saga of CONAN, following CONAN OF AQUILONIA (in preparation)." Lancer folded before publishing CONAN OF AQUILONIA; and the Conan novels were tied up in lawsuits until 1977, when Ace issued its series.

Thus, the first publication of CONAN OF AQUILONIA in book form is in the Ace series. (L. Sprague de Camp and Lin Carter had published it in four serials in FANTASTIC MAGAZINE.) Although it is number 11 in the chronology, it was the last book published in the Ace series. It is also the only volume in the series that does not appear in the uniform cover format. Since Lancer never published CONAN OF AQUILONIA, Ace had to commission its own cover painting--a very effective one by Boris Vallejo. But the new painting alone does not explain why the format of a two-and-a-half inch strip of white at the top of the cover, containing the title and all the copy, and appearing above the cover painting, was not followed. All the John Duillo covers were replaced by Boris Vallejo paintings; but, nevertheless, the other books are in the same Ace format.

An exception to the replacement of Duillo paintings with Boris ones is the last volume in the chronology, CONAN OF THE ISLES (Ace 11681). The first issue uses the Lancer cover painting by John Duillo, which shows a brawny Conan fighting a large snake that seems to have an artificial red tongue hanging out. L. Sprague de Camp and Lin Carter, authors of the pastiche, objecting to the nearly cartoonish appearance of the snake, persuaded Ace to have a new cover painted by Boris. The Boris painting appears on the later issue of the edition; but unlike

CONAN OF AQUILONIA, this variant issue is in
the standard format.

Another variant Conan paperback exists in
the Ace series: a copy with the cover of CONAN
THE AVENGER containing the text of CONAN THE
CONQUEROR. Loay Hall, as well as some other
collectors, has a copy of CONAN THE AVENGER
that prints the correct text up to the last
part of chapter XX. Part of chapter XX and all
of chapters XXI and XXII of CONAN THE CONQUEROR
were printed instead of the concluding chapters
of CONAN THE AVENGER.

Although the Lancer and Ace series contain
more Conan titles than are offered by any other
publisher, new pastiches have recently been
offered by Bantam. The most recent, of course,
is the novelization of the movie, CONAN THE
BARBARIAN, done by L. Sprague de Camp, Catherine
de Camp, and Lin Carter. Bantam published CONAN
THE LIBERATOR by de Camp and Carter in February
1979. It features a foldout cover by Bob Larkin,
to which de Camp strongly objected. Conan sits
on his throne while nearly naked women crawl
around at his feet in various poses of obeisance.
De Camp protested that the cover would be more
appropriate for a book titled "Conan the En-
slaver." In August of 1978, Bantam had published a de Camp/Bjorn Nyberg pastiche, CONAN
THE SWORDSMAN, with a cover by Darral Greene.

In 1982, Bantam is reissuing the books
with new covers; CONAN THE SWORDSMAN has a
cover by Zorin. The new cover shows Conan
swinging a sword against a host of enemies instead of merely being poised for action as on
the earlier cover. He also looks younger and
less demented on the new cover; and the back-
ground gives the feeling of cool, northern land-
scapes which Howard talked about, whereas the
earlier cover gave the feeling of a volcanic
explosion in a desert wasteland. However, one
wonders why everyone on the new cover is prac-

John Diullo

Boris

Conan The Freebooter

Lancer Edition   **Ace Edition**

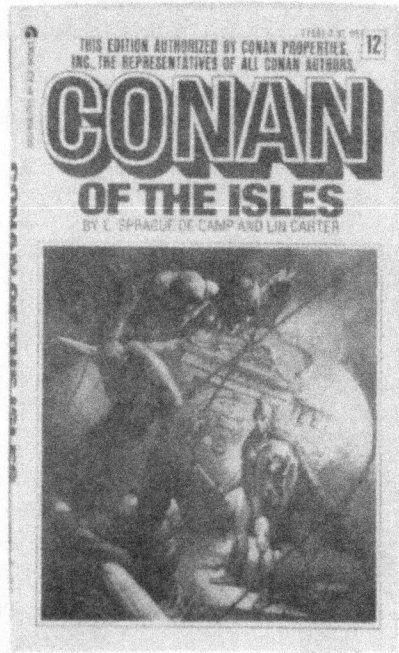

John Diullo

Boris

Conan of the Isles

Lancer Edition   **Ace Edition**

tically nude on all that ice. Perhaps the
Barbarian is immune to frostbite, but what
about his enemies and the distressed damsel?

The completist collector of Conan will
want not only all the Conan paperbacks, but
also those about Conan or using the name Conan
to promote sales of other books by Robert E.
Howard. Such a collection will include books
published by Dell, Berkley Medallion, Zebra,
Centaur, and Tempo (comic strip Conan in paperback form). Marvel Illustrated Books has also
issued a comic strip version of the movie in
paperback; its cover has a scene similar to
that of the movie posters and the novelization
of CONAN THE BARBARIAN. And since Berkley has
recently purchased Ace books the chronological
series of 12 volumes will probably be republished soon in a new edition.

A complete Conan collection will include
pastiches by Poul Anderson, Andrew Offutt, and
Karl Edward Wagner, as well as those by de Camp
and Carter. And at least one trade paperback
will have to be admitted to the completist's
collection: THE LAST CELT by Glenn Lord, a bio-
bibliography of Robert E. Howard, published in
1976 as a Berkley Windhover Book. Since so
many of the Conan novels and collections about
Howard are edited by L. Sprague de Camp and so
many of the pastiches were written by him, the
completist Conan collector might also want a
copy of Dan Levack's and my bibliography of de
Camp, which is to be published by Underwood/
Miller Publishers this October and contains
summaries by Loay Hall of all de Camp's works.
A copy can be ordered from Chuck Miller; 239
North Fourth Street; Columbia, Pennsylvania
17512.

[1]Karl Edward Wagner, Afterword, THE HOUR OF
THE DRAGON. (New York: Berkley Medallion, 1977).
[2]Paul M. Sammon, "Filming Robert E. Howard's
Sword and Sorcery Epic," CINEFANTASTIQUE, 12,2&3.

Following are lists of the two Lancer series and a complete list of the Ace series.

First Lancer Series

1. CONAN THE ADVENTURER #73-526 1966 (60¢)
   "Volume One of the Complete Conan" Cover by Frazetta
2. CONAN THE WARRIOR   #73-549 1967 (60¢)
   "Volume Two..." Cover by Frazetta
3. CONAN THE CONQUEROR   #73-572 1967 (60¢)
   "Volume Three..." Cover by Frazetta
4. CONAN THE USURPER   #73-599 1967 (60¢)
   "Volume Four..." Cover by Frazetta
5. CONAN   #73-685 1967 (60¢)
   "Volume Five..." Cover by Frazetta
6. CONAN THE AVENGER   #73-780 1968 (60¢)
   Not seen.   Cover by Frazetta
7. CONAN OF THE ISLES   #73-8000 1968 (60¢)
   No volume number. Cover by John Duillo.
8. CONAN THE FREEBOOTER   #74-963 1968 (75¢)
   No volume number. Cover by John Duillo.
9. CONAN THE WANDERER   #74-976 1968 (95¢)
   Not seen. Cover by John Duillo.
10. CONAN OF CIMMERIA   #75-072 1969 (95¢)
    Not seen. Cover by John Duillo.
11. CONAN THE BUCCANEER   #75-181 1971 (95¢)
    No volume number on the cover; but the title-page says, "Number Eleven in the Lancer Uniform Edition of CONAN. Chronologically this volume is Number Six in the Saga of CONAN, following CONAN THE ADVENTURER and preceding CONAN THE WARRIOR." Cover by Frazetta.

Second Lancer Series

1. CONAN   #75104 1970 (95¢)
   "Volume One of the Saga of Fantasy-Adventure's Mightiest Hero" Cover by Frazetta, as #5 above.
2. CONAN OF CIMMERIA   #75072 1970 (95¢)

"Volume Two..." Cover by Frazetta, as #10 above. While this printing is not given a new number, the cover, unlike #10 above, is redesigned in the new format.

3. CONAN THE FREEBOOTER #75119 1970 (95¢) "Volume Three..." Cover by Duillo, as #8 above.

4. CONAN THE WANDERER #74976 1970 (95¢) "Volume Four..." While this book is not given a number different from that of the 1968 printing (#9 above), it is in the new format.

5. CONAN THE CONQUEROR #75137 1970 (95¢) "Volume Five..." Cover by Frazetta, as #3 above.

6. CONAN OF THE ISLES #75136 1970 (95¢) "Volume Six..." Cover by Duillo, as #7 above.

7. CONAN THE WARRIOR #75148 1970 (95¢) "Volume Seven..." Cover by Frazetta, as #2 above.

8. CONAN THE AVENGER #75149 1970 (95¢) "Volume Eight..." Cover by Frazetta, as #6 above.

I have not seen a copy of the book immediately preceding CONAN (75104), the first volume in the new series. That book is CONAN THE USURPER (#75103); however, I have seen that #75102, CONAN THE ADVENTURER, is still in the original format with the number from the first series.

Volumes in both series were reprinted several times, but I did not include them in the lists unless they indicated a change in the numbering of the series. I would appreciate additions and corrections to these lists. I would also like to know if the Lancer copies printed 1971 to 1973 were numbered in the chronological order given below.

All volumes in the Ace chronological series were published in 1977. Unless otherwise noted the covers of the Ace editions are the same as those of the Lancer editions.

Ace Chronological Series

1.	CONAN	#11671	Howard, de Camp, Carter
2.	CONAN OF CIMMERIA	#11672	Howard, de Camp, Carter
3.	CONAN THE FREEBOOTER new cover by Boris	#11673	Howard, de Camp
4.	CONAN THE WANDERER new cover by Boris	#11674	Howard, de Camp, Carter
5.	CONAN THE ADVENTURER	#11675	Howard, de Camp
6.	CONAN THE BUCCANEER	#11676	de Camp, Carter
7.	CONAN THE WARRIOR	#11677	Howard, edited by de Camp
8.	CONAN THE USURPER	#11678	Howard, de Camp
9.	CONAN THE CONQUEROR	#11679	Howard, edited by de Camp
10.	CONAN THE AVENGER	#11680	Howard, Nyberg, de Camp
11.	CONAN OF AQUILONIA Cover by Boris Vallejo.	#11682	de Camp, Carter
12a.	CONAN OF THE ISLES	#11681	de Camp, Carter
b.	"	" " "	"

new cover by Boris Vallejo

OTHERGATES
1025 55th St.
Oakland, CA 94608

OTHERGATES is a semi-annual markets list in the fields of science fiction and fantasy, intended mainly for the use of writers and artists looking for places to publish their work. This unique publication includeds professional and small press markets. Send all queries to the above address and please include S.A.S.E.

The Paperback Dr. John Thorndyke
by Daniel G. Roberts

One of the more distressing puzzles for an early twentieth-century detective fiction enthusiast is the apparent unsuitability of such turn-of-the-century material to the American mass-market paperback audience. While Dover Publications' recent excellent series on early detective fiction and Penguin's Sherlock Holmes "Rivals" series, edited by Hugh Greene, are admirable attempts at filling this void, only the Penguin series, limited to four volumes of collected short stories, has apparently reached a relatively wide audience. Accordingly, many noteworthy turn-of-the-century authors are not readily available to the contemporary mystery-reading public. One of the best of the early twentieth-century detective fiction writers for which paperback editions are sadly lacking is R. Austin Freeman, whose most notable contributions center upon the Dr. John Thorndyke series, in which the art of ratiocination, in the incomparable tradition of Sherlock Holmes, is honed to a fine scientific edge.

Richard Austin Freeman was born on April 11, 1862, the son of a London tailor. A man with eclectic interests, but with a decided penchant for the arts and natural sciences, Freeman began a career in medicine at the age of eighteen at Middlesex Hospital. Shortly after receiving his medical degree in 1887, but without sufficient funds to open up his own practice, he found himself in the service of the British Government as an assistant Colonial Surgeon in the Gold Coast of Africa. After a stay of a little over a year in Accra, Gold Coast, Freeman spent some time as a medical officer and surveyor in the town of Bontuku, in West Africa but, by 1889, was back in Accra and

A DR. THORNDYKE MYSTERY

MR. POLTON EXPLAINS

R. AUSTIN FREEMAN

POPULAR LIBRARY

Mr. Polton Explains by R. Austin Freeman
Popular Library #70

resuming his original medical duties there,
where, in 1891, he became afflicted with black-
water fever, a disease that so debilitated him
that by 1896, he was forced to abandon his medical career. While these circumstances were un-
fortunate with regard to his own plans, the mis-
fortune which befell him had one lasting benefi-
cial effect on the rest of the world--the forced
inactivity brought on by the effects of his ill-
ness was the major impetus behind the launching
of Freeman's literary career. While certainly
not limited to the Thorndyke stories, nor to
detective fiction in general, Freeman's lasting
association as a writer is with Dr. John Thorndyke.

John Evelyn Thorndyke, like R. Austin Freeman, was a medical man; but, unlike Freeman,
Thorndyke was also a barrister-at-law. As an
amateur sleuth, he combined his legal and medical training into a personage of willful domi-
nance, impeccable logic, and scholarly and com-
prehensive inductive reasoning. By all accounts,
Thorndyke is the handsomest of all fictional
detectives, and every bit as dapper a gentleman
as the more popular Lord Peter Wimsey or Philo
Vance.

While Thorndyke's early upbringing remains
a mystery, we do know that he was born on July
4, 1870, thereby post-dating Freeman's own birth-
date by eight years. By the mid-1890s, Thorndyke
had received his M.D. and D.S.C. degrees from
St. Margaret's Hospital in London, and had begun
his medical career at the same institution in
various appointive positions. During this time,
he became interested in medical jurisprudence
and, by 1897, was applying his medical skills
as a defense attorney. It is unclear how
Thorndyke was able to be admitted to the bar so
shortly after acquiring his medical degrees,
especially since he appears to have had no
formal legal training, but practice law he

nevertheless did. It was Thorndyke's dual interests in medicine and the law, however, which
ultimately led him to combine both experience
and training into his own peculiar brand of
scientific ratiocinative inquiry.

Without doubt, Thorndyke's most famous and
recognizable trademark is his small canvas-
covered traveling case. Time and time again
throughout the stories and novels, Thorndyke
would extract from this case some obscure, yet
obviously necessary, scientific device to aid
him at the scene of the crime or back in his
laboratory. One of the most celebrated abilities
of the marvelous devices contained in his case
is the timely creation of plaster casts of foot-
prints at the scene of the crime.

Like most fictional detectives, Thorndyke
does not work alone. In fact, Thorndyke is
blessed with not one, but two able assistants,
in the personages of Nathaniel Polton and
Christopher Jervis. The talents of both men are
indispensible to Thorndyke, the former primarily
to attend to Thorndyke's more practical needs
and the latter to serve more as a passive confidant than as an active participant in his adventures.

Nathaniel Polton was rescued as an orphan
by Thorndyke, given room at his house (No.5A
King's Bench Walk), and became singularly devoted to Thorndyke as the years passed. It is
Polton, really, who is the mastermind behind
much of Thorndyke's successes, for it is in his
laboratory that Polton, a man of great mechanical genius and a jack-of-all trades, spends most
of his waking hours inventing, improving upon,
and reinventing many of Thorndyke's scientific
and mechanical devices which became so useful
for the solution of crimes. In later years,
Polton began to take on manservant duties; but
it is clearly as an inventor and all-purpose
handyman that he is indispensible to Thorndyke.

Early Avon Editions

Popular Library Editions

Christopher Jervis, it seems, rather than serving a fundamental first-hand purpose throughout the adventures, is a personage created principally for purposes of literary accomodation. Jervis is that seldom seen or heard accomplice whose primary duties are to serve as confidant to the great Thorndyke, and to record the facts of Thorndyke's affairs for posterity. Obviously, Jervis is to Thorndyke as Watson is to Sherlock Holmes, and his cerebral faculties seem to be nearly as suspect as those of Watson. Poor Jervis suffers the same fate as Watson throughout all of Thorndyke's adventures; that is, he is always in the dark until Thorndyke is ready to unveil his theories and solutions. Indeed, because of a Freeman innovation, the inverted story, Jervis is the only one who remains ignorant of the solution until well nigh the end.

While not detracting from his creation of the first scientific investigator in detective fiction, Freeman's most notable contribution to the genre was the "inverted story." In this literary form the reader, through the third person, is allowed to witness the crime as it is being committed at the outset of the story. In most of Freeman's inverted stories, an entire first section is devoted to this third person narration in which the reader witnesses the crime. The second part of the story is then related by Christopher Jervis; and, through the eyes of Jervis, the reader observes how Thorndyke applies his great inductive and scientific abilities to the identification and apprehension of the culprit. This literary form is, to say the least, a remarkable one, one which Freeman himself was not certain at the outset would be viable. Great narrative skill is needed in order to keep the reader's interest and, although there have been later imitators of the "inverted" style, Freeman alone stands as not only the ori-

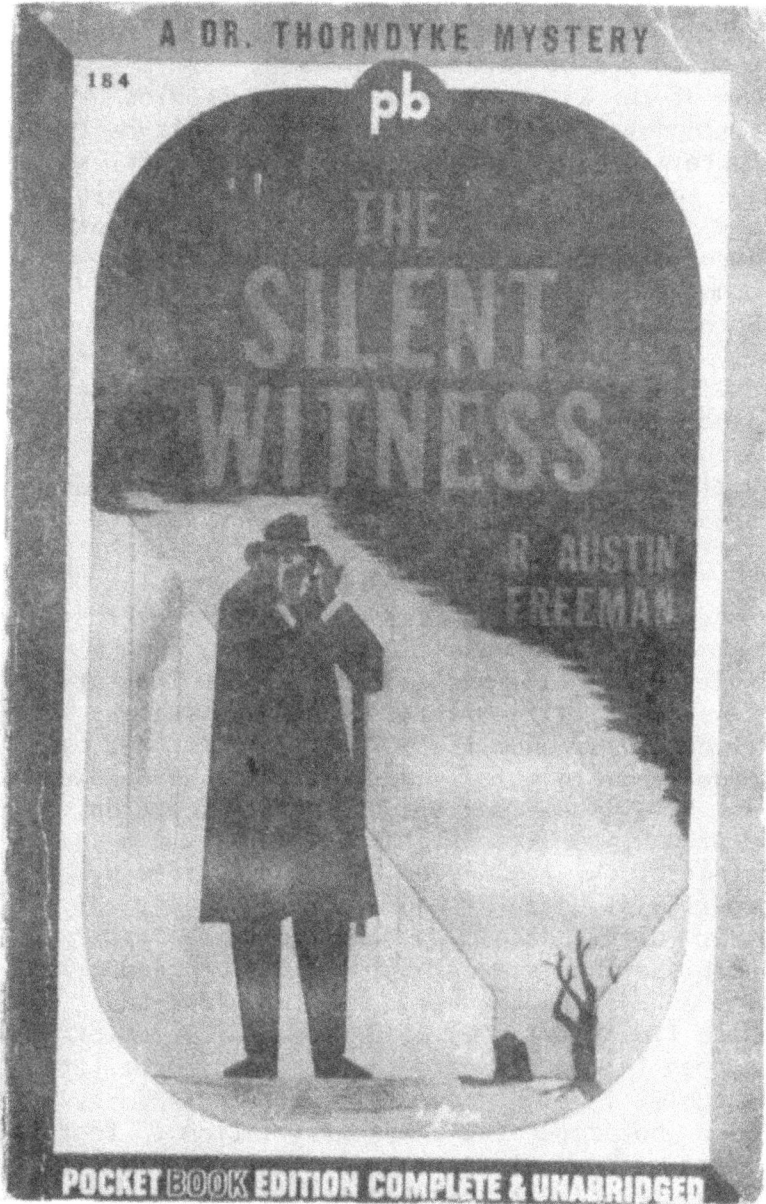

The Silent Witness by R. Austin Freeman
Pocket Book #184
Pocket Book's only Freeman title

ginator, but as the most successful proponent
of this form of detective fiction.

Of the 21 novels and 42 short stories
written by Freeman with Thorndyke as his central
figure, only six novels and ten short stories
have seen print in paperback editions. (This
does not include the occasional appearance of
Thorndyke in a paperback detective fiction
anthology.) In all, nine paperback editions of
Thorndyke have been printed and, of those nine,
only two (both Dover editions noted below) are
still in print. The following is a brief anno-
tated enumeration of the paperback editions of
R. Austin Freeman, as well as three limited
edition paperback entries of associational interest, including two pastiches and one biography.

DR. THORNDYKE'S DISCOVERY, Avon 10 (no
number, 1941) This novel represents the first
Freeman title to appear in paperback, and the
first of two to appear under the Avon imprint.
It is probably the rarest Freeman paperback. It
was originally published in Britain in 1932 by
Hodder and Stoughton under the title WHEN ROGUES
FALL OUT. The cover art of the Avon edition,
created by an unknown artist, features a grand-
father clock with hidden wall safe framed by
two figures, one in shadow holding a gun, the
other in full detail on hands and knees, presumably either searching for clues or recovering
from a knock on the head. A fine black-and-
white line drawing by J. B. Musacchia, depicting
two men in what appears to be a soon-to-be fatal
struggle, is also provided as a frontispiece.
Those who prefer their mystery fiction to feature
numerous seemingly unrelated threads will revel
in this classic Thorndyke story.

THE UNCONSCIOUS WITNESS, Avon 122 (1947)
Originally published in 1942 by Hodder and
Stoughton under the title THE JACOB STREET

MYSTERY, Dodd Mead issued the U. S. edition in the same year with the title used by Avon. It is the last Thorndyke tale written by R. Austin Freeman and by now, Thorndyke has surpassed his seventieth birthday. The paperback cover features an ornate border, typical of many Avon titles of 1946-1947, framing a tuxedoed and mustachioed gent aiding a comely damsel in distress as he fires away with his automatic pistol (certainly a misrepresentation of Thorndyke, if it is intended as such). The story, of course, is considerably more soft-boiled than the cover suggests. Thorndyke, however, is at his analytical best in this adventure, which may appeal to those relish "artsy" overtones to their mystery fiction.

THE SILENT WITNESS, Pocket Book 184 (1942) This novel represents the only Freeman title to appear in a Pocket Book edition, and the second Freeman title to appear in paperback. It was originally published in England by Hodder and Stoughton in 1914, and in the U. S. by John C. Winston in 1915 under the title A SILENT WITNESS. The copyright page of the Pocket Book edition erroneously indicates that Dood Mead's 1929 edition was the first printing. It features an intriguing cover by Hoffmann of a man, complete with trenchcoat and fedora, lighting a cigarette and framed by a barren streetscape. Christopher Jervis, Thorndyke's able narrator and confidant, takes a more direct role in this novel than in most.

THE STONEWARE MONKEY, Popular Library 11 (1943) This title is the first Freeman to appear in Popular Library's early "Mysteries of Proven Merit" series and, as the number implies, is the eleventh in the series. It reprints in an unabridged state a novel of the same title first published in Great Britain by Hodder and

Stoughton in 1938, and later in the United States by Dodd Mead in 1939. An admirable depiction by Hoffman of a sculptured monkey dripping blood, presumably not his own, adorns the front cover, while a photographic portrait of Freeman, as well as a short biographical statement, is featured on the back. The novel reveals an interesting use to which a pottery kiln can be put by one with devious intent.

MR. POLTON EXPLAINS, Popular Library 70 (1946) MR. POLTON EXPLAINS is the second Freeman title in the Popular Library series, and reprints an abridged version of the novel first published in 1940 by Hodder and Stoughton in England and by Dodd.Mead in the United States. The cover art is typical of the highly stylized depictions which adorned most early Popular Library editions and features a large clock and a man stealthily absconding with a box under his arm. The novel is sure to delight all those interested in horology.

THE ADVENTURES OF DR. THORNDYKE, Popular Library 122 (1947) This fine collection of short stories is the last of three Popular Library Freeman titles, and reprints the same stories originally published by Hodder and Stoughton in 1912 under the title THE SINGING BONE. The collection was not released in the United States until 1923, when Dood Mead issued it. There are five sotries in this collection, including "The Case of Oscar Brodski," "A Case of Premeditation," "The Echo of a Mutiny," "A Wastrel's Romance," and "The Old Lag." Each story features a division into two parts and represents typical "inverted" detective stories pioneered by Freeman, with "The Singing Bone" being the second part of "The Echo of a Mutiny." The stories are prefaced by a short introduction written at Gravesend by Freeman, presumably in

34

1912, in which he outlines his philosophy behind
the inverted stories. Cover art is by Fiedler,
and features a highly stylized depiction of a
distant lighthouse framed in the foreground by
a man wielding a stick or rod.

MR. POTTERMACK'S OVERSIGHT, Collier AS416Y
(1962) First published in 1930 by Hodder and
Stoughton in England and Dodd Mead in the United
States, this classic Thorndyke tale was entered
by Collier into its fine series of mystery fiction in 1962. It is the only Freeman story
published by Collier and, with the exception of
those titles issued by Dover, the last released
by an American paperback publisher. It features
a nondescript stylized depiction of a man, presumably a corpse, lying in a bed of leaves or
flowers. Like most other Collier titles, the
cover art leaves much to be desired. Those who
like their fictional criminals on the warm and
loveable side will find this Thorndyke title of
interest.

THE BEST DR. THORNDYKE DETECTIVE STORIES,
Dover 20388-3 (1973) This collection of eight
Thorndyke short stories was first published by
Dover Publications in 1973, and features an
introduction by E. F. Bleiler. Among them are
three "inverted" stories from THE SINGING BONE
(later titled THE ADVENTURES OF DR. THORNDYKE,
as noted earlier), including "The Case of Oscar
Brodski," "A Case of Premeditation," and "The
Echo of a Mutiny." Also presented are four
stories from John Thorndyke's Cases, published
in Britain by Chatto and Windus in 1909 (U. S.
title, DR. THORNDYKE'S CASES, Dodd Mead, 1931),
including "The Mandarin's Pearl," "The Blue
Sequin," "The Moabite Cipher," and "The Aluminum
Dagger." The anthology closes with "31 New Inn,"
first published by Hodder and Stoughton in 1912.
According to Bleiler, this short version may
represent the first Thorndyke story, with some

evidence indicating it may have been written as
early as 1905. It was first published in New
York in the January 1911 issue of ADVENTURE MAG-
AZINE, having never been published in England.
The cover of the Dover edition bears an interesting photograph of a turn-of-the-century urban
streetscape, presumably London, and was designed
by Edmund V. Gillon, Jr.

TWO DR. THORNDYKE DETECTIVE NOVELS: THE
STONEWARE MONKEY AND THE PENROSE MYSTERY, Dover
22963-7 (1973) As a companion volume to THE
BEST DR. THORNDYKE DETECTIVE STORIES, Dover
also published in 1973 two Freeman novels,
including one (THE PENROSE MYSTERY) which does
not appear in any other paperback edition. The
second novel, THE STONEWARE MONKEY, first appeared in paperback as Number 11 in the Popular
Library series, as noted earlier. THE PENROSE
MYSTERY was first published simultaneously in
1936 by Hodder and Stoughton in Britain and
Dodd Mead in the United States. The Dover
edition of these two novels features an informative introduction by E. F. Bleiler, as well
as a striking black-and-white photograph of the
stoneware monkey designed by Edmund V. Gillon,
Jr. Interestingly, and doubtless not coinci-
dentally, the Gillon rendition of the monkey is
remarkably similar to the Hoffman version on
the cover of the Popular Library edition of
THE STONEWARE MONKEY. For those who like their
mysteries with a decided archeological flavor,
THE PENROSE MYSTERY will nicely fill the bill.
According to Bleiler's introduction, in fact,
this story was influential in the funding of an
actual archeological excavation at Windmill Hill
in Britain.

Three additional titles of associational
interest to Freeman enthusiasts have also made
their appearance in paperbound editions, although none were released by mass-marketing

36

publishing houses. All three made their appearances in the early 1970s in limited editions, and all three, I believe, are currently out-of-print. Two represent pastiches, and one is a superlative biography, as described in the following paragraphs.

Pastiche: Donaldson, Norman; GOODBYE, DR. THORNDYKE, Luther Norris (1972) This is the first known Thorndyke pastiche to make its way into print. and represents a story admirably written in the style of Freeman by his biographer and chief proponent, Norman Donaldson. Donaldson was evidently perturbed that Freeman's last novel, THE UNCONSCIOUS WITNESS, did not serve as a fitting conclusion for the retirement years of the great detective, so he set about to suitably rectify the situation. In GOODBYE, DR. THORNDYKE, the setting is war-torn London of 1940-41, with the Honourable Society of the Inner Temple figuring prominently in the story. Embezzlement is the name of the game in this pastiche, and a series of puzzling threads wind their way through the novelette in a manner worthy of Freeman himself. The volume is handsomely produced by Luther Norris and includes a line drawing of Thorndyke as an elderly man on both the cover and the frontispiece. Other interior illustrations include a line drawing of the Inner Temple showing buildings destroyed by the "Blitz of London," a charcoal drawing by Peggy Eagle of a white-haired Thorndyke, a photograph of the Inner Temple Library and Clock Tower after the bombing in 1940, and a line drawing of No. 5A King's Bench Walk. All in all, this handsome little volume will delight all Thorndyke enthusiasts.

Pastiche: Dirck, John H.; DR. THORNDYKE'S DILEMMA, Aspen Press (1974) This title represents the second and last known Dr. Thorndyke pastiche in paperback and, although written in

admirable fashion, falls somewhat short of the
standards set in Donaldson's pastiche and, of
course, Freeman's tales themselves. Although
Donaldson intended for his pastiche to be the
last Thorndyke story, Dirck nevertheless saw
fit to continue the saga. The short novel
benefits significantly from the personal exper-
tise and experience of the author, who serves
as the medical director of the student health
center at the University of Dayton. In this
tale, Thorndyke has achieved the age of eighty
and although his penchant for deduction with
the aid of his scientific instruments and know-
ledge has not waned, he appears to preoccupy
himself with earlier memories, particularly
those of his since-departed assistant Polton.
The novel is marginally enhanced by two line
drawings by Rob Pudin and, although well-written
and highly entertaining, can probably best be
appreciated by hard-core Thorndyke devotees
only.

Biography: Donaldson, Norman; IN SEARCH
OF DR. THORNDYKE, Bowling Green University
Popular Press (1971) Heretofore, this exhaus-
tively researched volume which appeared as a
first edition trade paperback, represented the
only biography of R. Austin Freeman and his fictional detective, John Thorndyke. Recently,
however, I have learned of another biography
published in Australia (R. AUSTIN FREEMAN: THE
ANTHROPOLOGIST AT LARGE, by Oliver Mayo) but,
since I am not familiar with it, I will not dis-
cuss it here. In Donaldson's biography, we
learn as much about Freeman and Thorndyke as
possible, given the paucity of primary and sec-
ondary information with which Donaldson had to
work. We also learn a bit about John J. Pitcairn,
who collaborated with Freeman under the pseudonym
"Clifford Ashdown" in writing of the rogue Romney
Pringle, another equally entertaining fictional
character stemming from Freeman's imagination.

(Pringle has paperback appearances few and far between, most notably two short story appearances in Hugh Greene's THE RIVALS OF SHERLOCK HOLMES, Penguin Books, 1971.) While the body of the biography is extremely entertaining, informative, and scholarly, Donaldson's real contribution lies in the exhaustive bibliographical information on Freeman provided as appendices, including a listing of all his works, fictional and non-fictional alike, a detailed description of all first edition Freeman titles, and a listing of Freeman articles and short stories appearing in CASSELL'S MAGAZINE between 1898 and 1906. All Freeman enthusiasts owe a special debt of gratitude to the exhaustive research which Donaldson has provided.

In summary, Freeman's Thorndyke stories offer the present-day reader a look at a unique contemporary of the master detective Sherlock Holmes. While any comparison between Thorndyke and Holmes would prove to be self-defeating, it nevertheless can be said that, in Thorndyke, Freeman has created a character worthy of the serious attention of all detective fiction buffs who have yet to make his acquaintance. It is only to be lamented that Freeman books are difficult and expensive to obtain in the first state or even in later hardback reprints. That American mass-market paperback houses never saw fit to reprint most of his titles (and still apparently are not contemplating it) only compounds the problems in making an acquaintance with Thorndyke and Freeman. While searching for more elusive titles, the easily obtainable Dover reprints make a good beginning.

References

Bleiler, E. F. "Introduction," TWO DR. THORN-DYKE NOVELS: THE STONEWARE MONKEY AND THE PENROSE MYSTERY. New York: Dover Publications, Inc., 1973.

_____. "Introduction," THE BEST DR. THORN-
DYKE STORIES. New York: Dover Publications,
Inc., 1973.

Donaldson, Norman. IN SEARCH OF DR. THORNDYKE.
Bowling Green, Ohio: Bowling Green University Popular Press, 1971.

Hancer, Kevin. THE PAPERBACK PRICE GUIDE.
Cleveland, Tennessee: Overstreet Publications, 1980.

Hill, M. C. PAPERBACKS CHECKLIST FOR COLLECTORS,
Vol. 1. Owensboro, Kentucky: Cook and
McDowell Publishers, 1980.

Hubin, Allen J. "Introduction," GOODBYE, DR.
THORNDYKE. Culver City, California: Luther
Norris, 1972.

_____. THE BIBLIOGRAPHY OF CRIME FICTION,
1749-1975. San Diego: University of California at San Diego Publishers, Inc., 1979.

PAPERBOUND BOOKS IN PRINT, 1955-1980. New York:
R. M. Bowker Co..

Reginald, Robert, and Michael R. Burgess.
CUMULATIVE PAPERBACK INDEX, 1939-1959.
Detroit: Gale Research Company, 1973.

_____

Alias Maxwell Grant
by Will Murray

Walter B. Gibson, writing as Maxwell Grant, was one of the undisputed kings of the pulp magazines. His enormous reputation centers around a single character in a single magazine, both of which were named "The Shadow."

Less well-known is his paperback career. It, too, is dominated by "The Shadow"--mostly in reprint--but Gibson also produced a number of paperback originals, many of them even today almost totally unknown.

Gibson's first paperback appearance was THE SHADOW AND THE VOICE OF MURDER, a reprint of the pulp novel, VOICE OF DEATH. It was published by the Los Angeles-based Bantam Books in two editions--one with a pulp-like cover, the other without cover illustration, in 1945. These were the types of semi-paperbacks sold mainly in Woolworth stores.

Around this time, Vital Publications began reissuing digest-sized reprints of the pulp Nick Carter novels, and Gibson was asked to revise these. He did, and this led to two original digest novels, A BLONDE FOR MURDER and LOOKS THAT KILL, both featuring magician-detectives as their leads.

In 1947, humorist Harry Hershfield was asked to novelize Harold Lloyd's last movie, THE SIN OF ROGER DIDDLEBOCK, for Bart House. Hershfield stalled out in the first chapter, and Gibson was asked to help. He wrote the complete novelization, ghosting it for Hershfield.

During the fifties, Gibson was writing extensively for the true crime magazines, and wrote three novels--based on fact--for a digest, CRIME CASE BOOK MAGAZINE. They were JOHN CHRISTIE AND HIS HOUSE OF DEATH by "John Abbington"; THE CASTLE OF HORRORS, under his real name; and THE

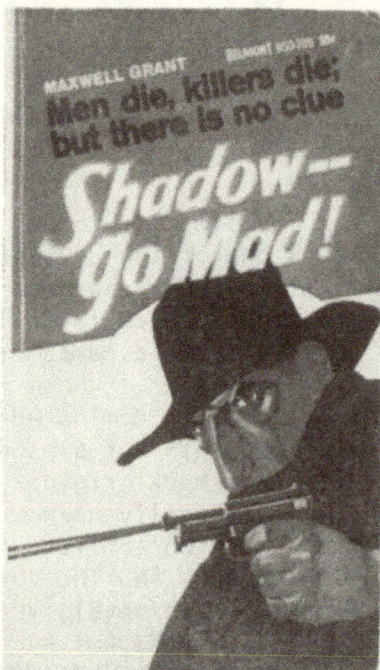

The Shadow (Belmont Editions)

The Shadow (Bantam Editions)

CORONATION MURDERS as "P. L. Raymond" in the
January, March and May, 1954 issues.

One of Gibson's oddest novels was the rather racy account of Anne Bonney's meeting with
Blackbeard in ANNE BONNEY, PIRATE QUEEN. Loosely
based on fact, and spiced up considerably, this
1962 Monarch Book was, as Gibson will tell you,
the only book he ever wrote that was officially
banned in the state of Maine.

The next year saw the RETURN OF THE SHADOW
under his own name for Belmont. This original
novel was intended to be followed up by pulp
reprints, but Belmont changed their minds and
Gibson refused to write more originals for the
low advances they were offering. Belmont then
got Dennis Lynds to write the character.

In 1963, Gibson edited a collection of
Shadow reprints for Grosset & Dunlap, as well
as writing two Twilight Zone collections. Tempo
Books later reprinted one Shadow, GROVE OF DOOM,
in severely abridged form. THE TWILIGHT ZONE
and TWILIGHT ZONE REVISITED claimed that the
stories were "adapted by Walter B. Gibson," but
these were original stories from Gibson's imagination.

The Shadow returned in reprint in 1969,
when Bantam Books, their Doc Savage reprints
going strong, began to reissue the novels. The
series did poorly, partially because of the
covers by Sanford Kossim and others and died in
1970, with two reprints, THE SILENT SEVEN and
THE CRIME CULT, scheduled for 1971. They never
appeared.

The Shadow was not dead in paperback, how-
ever. Pyramid Books began a new reprint series
in 1974, reissuing THE LIVING SHADOW (which was
Bantam's first reprint title) and doing 22
other unreprinted novels, including the two
Bantams never produced. Covers by artist James
Steranko helped sales; and, when Pyramid became
Jove, the books kept coming out. In fact, there

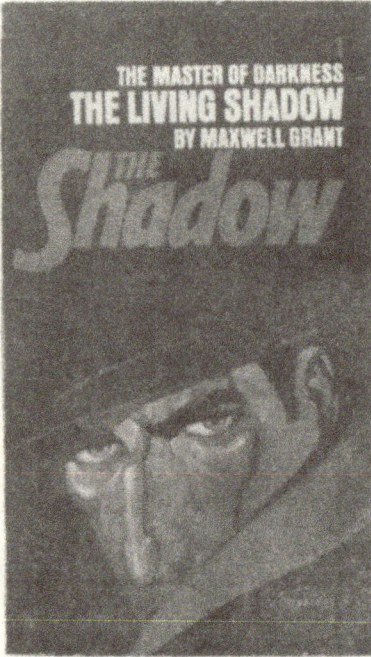

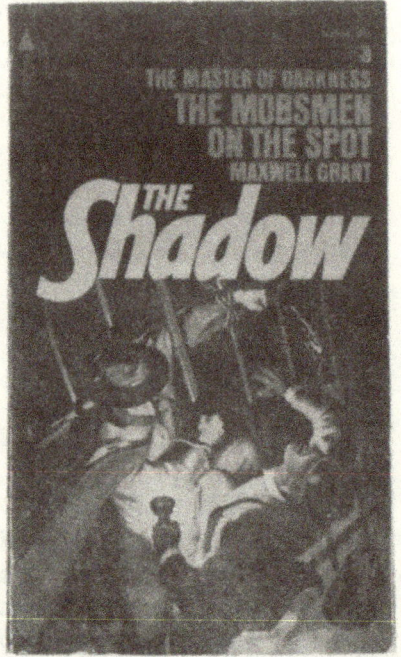

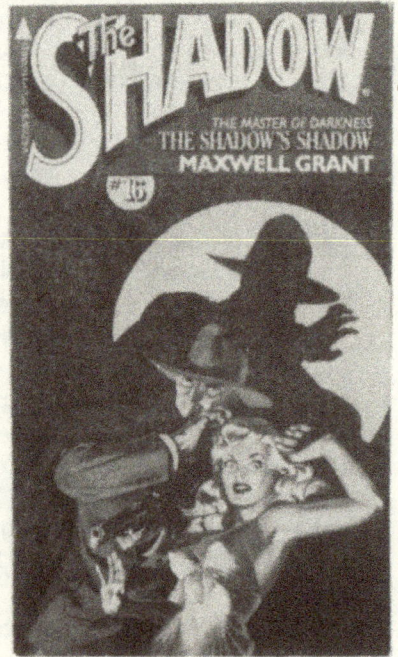

were several editions of this series, including variant covers of special note.

When they were first printed, HANDS IN THE DARK and THE CRIME CULT, accidentally appeared with each other's covers. They were later reprinted with the proper covers, making an interesting quartet of books. THE MOBSMEN ON THE SPOT featured an original pulp cover by George Rozen, instead of a Steranko cover. Rozen, who created The Shadow pictorially, died in 1974; and, as a tribute, Steranko allowed Rozen's cover for the May 1, 1942 SHADOW to be used, with the proceeds going to Rozen's widow. Four Jove editions were reprinted with new Steranko covers--THE LIVING SHADOW, THE ROMANOFF JEWELS, KINGS OF CRIME and SHADOWED MILLIONS. A new cover was painted for a reissue of GREEN EYES, but Jove killed the series before it appeared. The reason was not poor sales. Sales were good; but these were the days when publishers aimed for blockbuster million-selling paperbacks, and The Shadow's sales were merely solid and steady.

For the moment, neither The Shadow nor Walter B. Gibson is appearing in paperback, but this may change. In fact, it is virtually assured to change. The Shadow is not likely to die after living so long already.

The Shadow in Paperback

THE SHADOW AND THE VOICE OF MURDER, by Maxwell Grant. (LA Bantam, #21, 1940?)
THE SIN OF ROGER DIDDLEBOCK, by Harry Hirshfield. (Bart House, 1947)
ANNE BONNEY, PIRATE QUEEN, by Douglas Brown. (Monarch, 1962)

Digest-Sized Paperbacks

LOOKS THAT KILL, by Walter B. Gibson. (Vital, 194)

A BLONDE FOR MURDER, by Walter B. Gibson.
   (Vital, 1946)
THE CASTLE OF HORRORS, by Walter B. Gibson.
   (CRIME CASE BOOK MAGAZINE, Vol. 1, No. 2,
   March 1954)
THE CORONATION MURDERS, by P. L. Raymond.
   (CRIME CASE BOOK MAGAZINE, Vol. 1, No. 3,
   May 1954)
JOHN CHRISTIE AND HIS HOUSE OF DEATH, by John
   Abbington. (CRIME CASE BOOK MAGAZINE, Vol.
   1, No. 1, January 1954)

Tempo Books

THE TWILIGHT ZONE, by Walter B. Gibson, no date.
TWILIGHT ZONE REVISITED, by Walter B. Gibson,
   1967
THE FINE ART OF SPYING, edited by Walter B.
   Gibson, 1967
GROVE OF DOOM, by Walter Gibson, 1969

Belmont Books

RETURN OF THE SHADOW, by Maxwell Grant, 1963.
   #90-298
THE SHADOW STRIKES, by Maxwell Grant,
   #92-602
SHADOW BEWARE, by Maxwell Grant,
   #92-615
CRY SHADOW, by Maxwell Grant,   . #92-624.
THE SHADOW'S REVENGE, by Maxwell Grant, 1965.
   #B50-647
MARK OF THE SHADOW, by Maxwell Grant,
   #B50-683
SHADOW--GO MAD!, by Maxwell Grant, 1966.
   #B50-709
THE NIGHT OF THE SHADOW, by Maxwell Grant,
   #B50-683
THE SHADOW: DESTINATION MOON, by Maxwell
   Grant, 1967. #B50-737

Bantam Books

THE LIVING SHADOW, by Maxwell Grant, 1969.
   #4463, Book #1 in the series.
THE EYES OF THE SHADOW, by Maxwell Grant,
   1969.
THE SHADOW LAUGHS!, by Maxwell Grant,
   1969.
THE DEATH TOWER, by Maxwell Grant, 1969.
THE GHOST MAKERS, by Maxwell Grant, 1970.
HIDDEN DEATH, by Maxwell Grant, 1970. #H4884,
   Book #6 in the series.
GANGDOM'S DOOM, by Maxwell Grant, 1970. #H5413,
   Book #7 in the series.

Pyramid/Jove Books
(all under the name Maxwell Grant)

#1 THE LIVING SHADOW (Pyramid N3597, 1974;
    Jove/HBJ V4576, 1977).
#2 THE BLACK MASTER (Pyramid N3478, 1974)
#3 THE MOBSMAN ON THE SPOT (Pyramid N3554, 1974).
#4 HANDS IN THE DARK (Pyramid 3557, 1975).
#5 DOUBLE Z (Pyramid N3700, 1975).
#6 THE CRIME CULT (Pyramid N3699, 1975).
#7 THE RED MENACE (Pyamid N3875, 1975).
#8 MOX (Pyramid N3876, 1975).
#9 THE RAMANOFF JEWELS (Pyramid N3877, 1975;
    Jove/HBJ V4617, 1977).
#10 THE SILENT SEVEN (Pyramid N3966, 1975).
#11 KINGS OF CRIME (Pyramid N3967, 1976;
    Jove/HBJ V4582, 1978).
#12 SHADOWED MILLIONS (Pyramid N3968, 1976;
    Jove HBJ V4615, 1978.
#13 GREEN EYES (Pyramid V4205, 1977).
#14 THE CREEPING DEATH (Pyramid V4206, 1977).
#15 GRAY FIST (Pyramid V4207, 1977; Jove/HBJ
    V4207, 1977).
#16 THE SHADOW'S SHADOW (Pyramid V4278, 1977).
#17 FINGERS OF DEATH (Jove/HBJ V4279, 1977).

```
#18 MURDER TRAIL (Jove/HBJ V4280, 1977).
#19 ZEMBA (Jove/HBJ V4285, 1977)
#20 CHARG, MONSTER (Jove/HBJ V4284, 1977).
#21 THE WEALTH SEEKER (Jove/HBJ V4283, 1978).
#22 THE SILENT DEATH (Jove/HBJ V4281, 1978).
#23 THE DEATH GIVER (Jove/HBJ V4282, 1978).

(#1,11,12,13, and 14 were also repainted.  All
except #13 were released in a very small edition.)
```

Paperback Quarterly currently needs non-fiction articles about paperback publishers, authors, artists, individual books, or series. All articles must be slanted toward the paperback connection. Payment: 2¢ per word; Reporting time: 8 weeks.

Letters

Dear Mr. Lee,

    Tell Al Grossman that the name of the artist who did the cover for THE GHOST DANCERS (Lancer 447-75239) is Charles Moll.

    Next in order, I would like to correct an error on my part and an error on your part which appeared in my letter. Gil Brewer's MEMORY OF PASSION (Lancer 70-008) was published in 1962, not 1963 as stated. Mea Culpa! I took this date from Allen J. Hubin's BIBLIOGRAPHY OF CRIME FICTION, but should have checked it with the book in my own collection. Allen Hubin has made many errors regarding the dates of publication of Lancer books. So my advice to those who use it is to check with a second source. The book number for Willo Davis Roberts' SINISTER GARDENS should read 447-75405. Tua culpa!

    In connection with Michael Barson's useful and informative checklist of Norman Daniels' paperback originals, I would like to add the following:

    DR. KILDARE'S SECRET ROMANCE (Lancer 70-007), 1962

    ROBERT TAYLOR'S DETECTIVES (Lancer 71-316), 1962

    DR. KILDARE'S FINEST HOUR (Lancer 70-32), 1963

    BEN CASEY: THE FIRE WITHIN (Lancer 70-045), 1963

    STRIKE FORCE (Lancer 72-904), 1965

    DARK DESIRE (Lancer 73-658), 1967

    A KILLING IN THE MARKET (Lancer 73-700), 1967

    One strange Lancer that I have is SAM BENEDICT: CAST THE FIRST STONE (Lancer 70-035), 1963. Both the cover and the spine list Norman Daniels as the author, but the title page states that it is by Elsie Lee.

Finally, from Bill Crider's article, "SF Writers in Other Fields," with regard to Asimov's A WHIFF OF DEATH, Lancer published this in 1969 (Lancer 74-545) with a 75¢ price on it. The copyright statement says that it was "originally published under the title:: THE DEATH DEALERS." The 95¢ issue (Lancer 447-75315) was published in 1972.

> Sincerely,
> Victor A. Berch, Special
> Collections Librarian
> Brandeis University

Dear PQ,

Jim Goodrich's letter reminds me of a couple of points in recent issues that I had intended to comment on. I'd better do so before I forget again.... Jim mentions William L. Hamling, who was also mentioned in the Robert Bloch interview in IV:1. Since Hamling was involved with a couple of paperback imprints which are now considered collectible (but isn't everything?), perhaps a little potted history might not be out of place.

Hamling was a science fiction fan in the 1930s, wrote some sf and fantasy sotries for the Ziff-Davis magazines in 1939-47, and was Associate Editor and later Managing Editor of AMAZING STORIES and FANTASTIC ADVENTURES under Ray Palmer. When Palmer left Ziff-Davis to found his own sf magazine, Hamling did likewise. From 1951 to 1958 he edited and published IMAGINATION and IMAGINATIVE TALES (later known as SPACE TRAVEL) from a basement office in his home on Greenleaf Avenue in Evanston, Illinois---hence the name Greenleaf Publishing Company. In 1955 he began a men's magazine named ROGUE, which was edited for several years by Frank M. Robinson, and published a lot of interesting material (mostly non-ficiton) by Bloch, Alfred Bester, and other sf writers.

In 1961 Greenleaf introduced the Regency
Books paperback imprint, originally under the
editorship of Harlan Ellison; Algis Budrys took
over as Editor-in-Chief after a few months. In
the interview with Robert Bloch in PQ IV:1,
Michael Barson refers to Regency as having "fail-
ed quickly." Well, "quickly" is a relative term:
Regency lasted for about two and a half years,
from June 1961 to late 1963. Bloch's FIREBUG
was the first Regency title, followed by Ellison's
GENTLEMAN JUNKIE. Many of the covers during the
first year were done by Lionel Dillon, which
alone makes the books worth seeking out. The
Regency line included non-sf work by a number of
familiar sf names: Robert Sheckley's adventure/
suspense novel THE MAN IN THE WATER: Philip José
Farmer's novel of an interracial love affair,
FIRE AND THE NIGHT; a biography of de Sade,
PHILOSOPHER OF EVIL; and a book on HOW TO SPEND
MONEY by Robert Silverberg, both under the pseudonym "Walter Drummond"; a collection of true-
crime articles, CRIMES AND CHAOS, by Avram David-
son; and a non-fiction book, THE RABBLE ROUSERS,
by Eric Frank Russell. The line also included
a couple of good sf novels, SOME WILL NOT DIE by
Algis Budrys and THE ELEVENTH COMMANDMENT by
Lester del Rey, as well as books by B. Travern,
Hal Ellson, David Alexander, and others.
     While the Regency line was growing, Hamling
was also involved (so I was told at the time)
with a prono imprint called Nightstand Books.
And in 1965 Hamling started the Greenleaf Classics imprint, to be devoted at first mostly to
"high class" erotica. The first GC title was
CANDY by "Maxwell Kenton," followed by an English
translation of Krafft-Efing's PSYCHOPATHIA SEXU-
ALIS. Next came seven volumes of Henry Miller,
and Jean Genet's THE THIEF'S JOURNAL.
     At this point Greenleaf Publishing Company
moved from Evanston, Illinois, to San Diego. The
original Regency line had come to an end, but the

name was carried along to California, along
with Greenleaf Classics. The latter imprint
continued as before, with occasional forays out-
side of the sex field, such as J. P. Donleavy's
THE GINGER MAN and a transcript of the 1966
Senate hearings on the Vietnam war, THE TRUTH
ABOUT VIETNAM.

In its second incarnation, Regency Books
published several series of reprints from the
single-character pulps of the late 1930s and
early 1940s: PHANTOM DETECTIVE (22 titles),
OPERATOR 5 (eight titles), DR. DEATH (three titles), SECRET AGENT X (seven titles), DUSTY
AYRES AND HIS BATTLE BIRDS (five titles), and
anthologies from the "shudder pulps" (three titles). All of these pulp reprints had interesting cover paintings by Robert Bonfils, and
make a nice collectible group. (I once had a
complete set, but--ulp!--gave the books away.
I've lost track of the number of times I've
kicked myself for that inexplicable act.) In
June 1966 a new imprint, Corinth Books, began to
be used on the pulp reprints. Corinth Publications, Inc., was one of several alternate names
under which the Hamling empire operated; others
were Phenix Publishers, Ltd., and Ember Library
Books. The imprints Leisure Books, Ember Library,
Companion Books, Adult Books, Idle Hour Books,
Late-Hour Library Books, Sundown Readers, and
who knows how many others, were strictly porno
imprints affiliated with the Hamling operation.

Some of the Regency books noted above would
qualify for inclusion in Bill Crider's article
on "SF Writers in Other Fields." Other candi-
dates: several Gothics by Marion Zimmer Bradley,
Leigh Brackett's two Westerns, a couple of Western movie novelizations by Theodore Sturgeon,
several other mystery/suspense novels by Jack
Vance in addition to BAD RONALD, Poul Anderson's
three detective novels, or his historical novels
(ROGUE SWORD,etc.), a private-eye novel by Keith

Laumer, and lots more. Not all of these have appeared in paperback form, however.

One item that doesn't qualify, however, is Fritz Leiber's THE SINFUL ONES, which is definitely sf (or science/fantasy). And although the 1980 Pocket Books edition was the first publication since 1953 of the complete novel, the short version, titled YOU'RE ALL ALONE, was published by Ace Books in 1972. At either length and under either name, it's a terrific book.

That's an ambitious (and tiring) publication schedule you plan. Don't let it exhaust you. A late PQ is far better than no PQ at all.

Best wishes,
Bob Briney
Salem, Massachusetts

Books About Books
by Charlotte Laughlin

Mass Market Publishing in America, edited by Allen Billy Crider. G. K. Hall, 1982. $35.00.

Under Cover: An Illustrated History of American Mass Market Paperbacks, by Thomas L. Bonn. Penguin, 1982. $12.95.

    Objectively reviewing books written or edited by contributing editors of PQ is difficult for me, even more so in these cases because the content of the books is of such great personal interest to me. In addition, I am delighted that association with PQ has helped Tom Bonn and Bill Crider to produce book-length studies of paperbacks. Bill Crider inscribed a book for Billy C. Lee, "To Billy--because if he hadn't gotten me involved with PQ I wouldn't have had the chance to do this book." Now that makes us think that maybe all the hassle and expense PQ has been to us in the past four years has been worthwhile!
    Since I cannot be objective, I will simply state my biases before going into the accolades I think these books deserve. I am particularly biased in favor of MASS MARKET PUBLISHING IN AMERICA because I wrote ten of the 68 articles; others were written by Mike Barson, another PQ contributing editor; still others by BoucherCon friends and acquaintances (Walter Albert, Ellen Nehr, George Kelly, and Guy Townsend; and others by Louis Black, founder of TEXAS PAPERBACK COLLECTORS NEWSLETTER, and by Lance Casebeer, editor of COLLECTING PAPERBACKS?, which assumed the subscription list of TPCN.
    MASS MARKET PUBLISHING IN AMERICA is an alphabetically arranged history of paperback

publishers--starting with Ace and going through
Zenith. It covers lesser known (and often short-
lived) publishers such as Anson Bond Publications,
Checkerbooks, Croydon Publishing Company, Hanro
Publications, Ideal Publications (using such
imprints as Black Knight, Green Circle, and
Green Dragon), Parsee Publications, Pony Books,
and Red Arrow Books as well as the giants of
paperback publishing. The index covers titles,
authors, and editors, as well as publishers.

One difficulty with any such reference
book is that the entries for present-day publishers soon become outdated. The research for
MASS MARKET PUBLISHING was complete in the
summer of 1980, but the book was not published
until the spring of 1982. In the meantime,
Fawcett has sold to Ballantine; and the Putnam
publishing group, which includes Berkley/Jove,
has purchased Grosset/Ace, which includes Charter
and Tempo Books. MASS MARKET PUBLISHING has
separate entries for Ace, Berkley, Charter, Jove,
and Tempo, covering the consolidation of Berkley
and Jove in 1979 and the purchase of Ace by
Charter Communications, a Grosset & Dunlap
company, in 1969. The reader need only be aware
that despite the 1982 copyright date, he is reading 1980 information. In addition, having
learned a little bit more about Croydon and Red
Arrow Books in the past two years, I wish that
the information could have been incorporated into
the text. I also wish that the copy editors had
been a little more careful. Saying that the
Library of Congress has the files of "the westers"
instead of the files of "Western Publishing
Company" renders the sentence senseless. And
the cover of Dell #84, GOLD COMES IN BRICKS, is
said to show a "baby" in a coffin rather than a
"body" in a coffin.

MASS MARKET PUBLISHING contains 42 full
page, black-and-white reproductions of paperbacks.
And though I would have liked G K. Hall to have

had more reproductions, the ones they feature
compliment the chapters nicely.

G. K. Hall intends MASS MARKET PUBLISHING
for the library trade and is not marketing it
through book stores, although you can get your
book store to special order it for you or order
it yourself from G. K. Hall (70 Lincoln Street,
Boston, Mass. 02111). Since it is intended for
the library trade, the 294-page book is very
sturdily bound and printed on acid-free paper--
hence the expensive price.

★ ★ ★

I am biased in favor of UNDER COVER not
only because Thomas Bonn is its author but also
because it is a beautifully designed oversize
trade paperback, with wide outer margins allow-
ing room for subtitles or for an occasional
photograph. Beth Tondreau, the book's designer,
did more than an average job with layout, it's
clever.

The front and back cover each features full-
color reproductions of paperbacks, ranging from
Pocket Books' first, THE GOOD EARTH, to THE
THORN BIRDS and FEAR OF FLYING. Inside are more
than 100 full-color photographs and numerous
black-and-whites. Reviewing the book in the
NEW YORK TIMES BOOK REVIEW, Ray Walters says
that he finds the black-and-whites to be somewhat fuzzy; but most of them are quite crisp
reproductions--no more than four of five of the
seventy some-odd black-and-white pictures are in
the least fuzzy, and those are not distractingly
so.

From the forward by famous bibliographer
John Tebbel, to the thorough index, UNDER COVER
is a model of scholarship delivered in a popular
style. Part I is a "Brief History" of paperback
publishing, beginning with the European prelude,
moving through the dime novels and penny dread-

fuls to Pocket Books and the consequent mush-
rooming of the paperback industry. This Part
concludes with entries for 12 of today's most
active paperback houses. Part II is devoted to
cover art and design, with sections on the art
director, cover artist, point of sale, evolution
of cover art, and genre. Part III is titled
"Collecting" and discusses approaches to collecting, cover art collecting and other collectible
features, care and condition of collectible
paperbacks, and finally some hints for "Future
Collectible Paperbacks."

Bonn's lists for further reading, divided
into historical and collecting, are also very
helpful. Overall, it's a wonderfully entertaining and informative book.

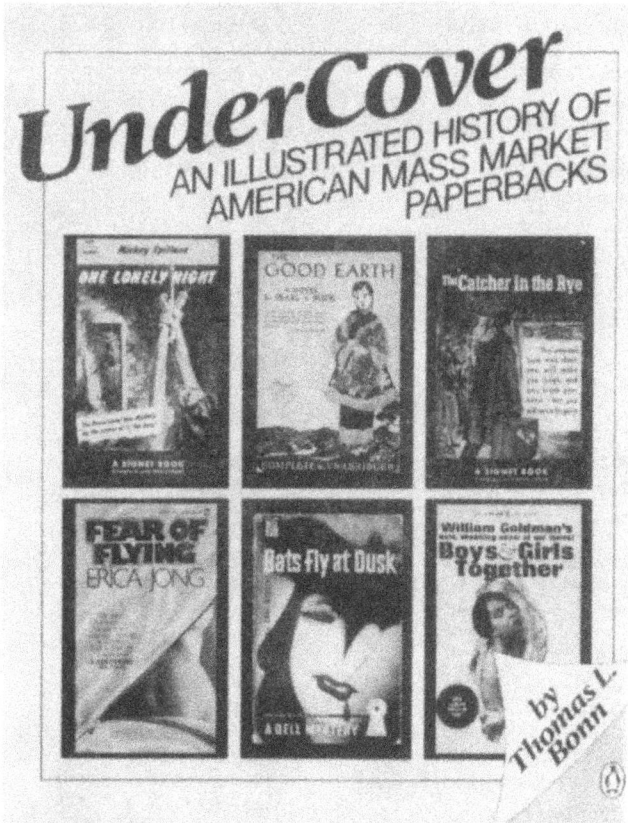

Book Sellers

The following people sell paperbacks. Many mail out booklists and all are knowledgeable paperback bibliophiles. For specific wants write directly to the addresses below and please include S.A.S.E.

BILL LYLES
77 High St.
Greenfield, MA 01301

Scott Owen
P.O. Box 343
Moraga, CA 94556

JEFF PATTON
3621 Carolina St., N.W.
Massillon, OH 44646

GRAVESEND BOOKS
Box 235
Poconopines, PA 18350

McCLINTOCK BOOKS
P.O. Box 3111
Warren, OH 44485

ANTHONY SMITH
1414 Lynnview Dr.
Houston, TX 77055

FANTASTIC WORLDS BOOKSTORE
4816 A Camp Bowie Blvd.
Fort Worth, TX 76107

PCI
P.O. Box 1308
Hawaiian Gardens, CA 97016

JOHN DA PRATO
61 Puffer Lane
Sudbury, MA 01776

FAMILY PAPERBACKS
4016 Central Ave. N.E.
Minneapolis, MN 55412

LONE WOLF MYSTERIES
160 Pennsylvania Ave.
Mt. Vernon, N.Y. 10552

RALPH KRISTIANSEN
P.O. Box 524-Kenmore Station
Boston, MA 02215

ED KALB
3227 E. Enid Ave.
Mesa, Arizona 85204

JEFF MEYERSON
50 First Place
Brooklyn, N.Y. 11231

MURDER BY THE BOOK
194½ Atwells Ave.
Providence, RI 02903

JACK IRWIN
16 Gloucester Lane
Trenton, N.J. 08618

THE OLD BOOK STORE
210 E. Cuyahoga Falls Ave.
Akron, OH 44310

FANTASY ARCHIVES
71 Eight Ave.
New York, N.Y. 10014

BILL LIPPINCOTT
Box 506
Bingham, ME 04920

THE ODYSSEY SHOP
1743 S. Union Ave.
Alliance, OH 44601

MICHAEL BARSON
117 Crosby St.
Haverhill, MA 01830

LARRY RICKERT
R.D. 1 Box 56C
Augusta, NJ 07822

SIGN OF THE UNICORN
604 Kingstown Rd.
Peace Dale, RI 02883

ABRA-CADAVER
110 Dunrovin Lane
Rochester, N.Y. 14618

BUNKER BOOKS
P.O. BOX 1638
Spring Valley, CA 92077

GALE SEBERT
Sebert's Books
Leivasy, WV 26676

RON CZERWIEN
7289 W. 173rd Pl.
Tinley Park, IL 60477

PANDORA'S BOOKS LTD
Box 86
Neche, ND 58265

DIAMOND LAKE BOOK STORE
1 West Diamond Lake Rd.
Minneapolis, Minn. 55419

JOHN HARTLING
1124 Galloway
Columbia, TN 38401

C.D. DUNCAN
Box 9802 Suite 122
Austin, TX 78766

BECKY ICAZA
33 Spring Park Ave.
Jamaica Plain, MA 02130

JACK'S BOOK SHOP
718 E. Northwest Hwy.
Mt. Prospect, IL 60056

20th CENTURY BOOKS
2501 University Ave.
Madison, WI 53705

TRACKER BOOKS
P.O. Box 8463
Salt Lake City, Utah
84108

COLE SPRINGER
P.O. Box 650
Times Square Station
New York, N.Y. 10108

REMEMBER WHEN SHOP
2433 Valwood Pkwy.
Dallas, TX 75234

LUCILE COLEMAN
P.O. Box 610813
North Miami, FL 33161

KEITH & MARTIN BOOK SHOP
310 W. Franklin St.
Chapel Hill, NC 27514

MOSTLY MYSTERIES BOOKS
398 St. Clair Ave. East
Toronto, Ontario M4T 1P5

TOM NIGRA
865 Diane Court
Woodbridge, NJ 07095

GORGON BOOKS
21 Deerlane
Wantagh, N.Y. 17793

BEASLEY BOOKS
1533 W. Oakdale, 2nd FL.
Chicago, IL 60657

R.C. & ELWANDA HOLLAND
302 Martin Dr.
Richmond, KY 40475

JOHN GARBARINO
118 Cedar Lane
Teaneck, NJ 07666

ATTIC BOOKS
908 Howard Place
Suffolk, VA 23434

INA COOKE/M.J. MUNRO
Unicorn Books
604 Kingston Rd.
Peace Dale, RI 02883

BARRY & WALLY PATTENGIL
The Book Bin
323 Parkdale Center
Waco, TX 76710

If you are bookseller and would like your name and address
printed in "Book Sellers," please drop us a line. Please tell
us if you sell paperbacks by mail and/or have a retail store.

www.ingramcontent.com/pod-product-compliance
Lightning Source LLC
Chambersburg PA
CBHW021224020426
42331CB00003B/457